The Leadership Touch

The Leadership Touch

The Search for a Rare Quality

What is it?
What causes it?
Why is it important?
How can you develop it?

John R. Hook

iUniverse, Inc.
New York   Bloomington

The Leadership Touch
The Search for a Rare Quality

iUniverse books may be ordered through booksellers or by contacting:

iUniverse
1663 Liberty Drive
Bloomington, IN 47403
www.iuniverse.com
1-800-Authors (1-800-288-4677)

Because of the dynamic nature of the Internet, any Web addresses or links contained in this book may have changed since publication and may no longer be valid. The views expressed in this work are solely those of the author and do not necessarily reflect the views of the publisher, and the publisher hereby disclaims any responsibility for them.

ISBN: 978-1-4401-3281-0 (pbk)
ISBN: 978-1-4401-3282-7 (ebk)

Printed in the United States of America

iUniverse rev. date: 4/6/2009

Dedicated
to
Caroline Grace Herrmann

My granddaughter and my hero. At age 13, with extraordinary courage and selfless love, she led us all through our most difficult days. Caroline defined the leadership touch and set the standard for a noble life. I will always seek to be guided by her example. God Bless!

"There's no other way but through."

Caroline's motto

Table of Contents

Acknowledgments

The following colleagues and friends provided views on attributes important to the leadership touch. Their reflections, informed by extensive experience, were invaluable and are recorded verbatim in Chapter 4.

Colonel Charles A. Beitz, Jr., USA (Ret.), DPA
Colonel George A. Bicher, USA (Ret.)
Dr. John W. Campbell
Dr. D. Kirk Davidson
John J. Dohony, Jr.
Dr. William G. Forgang
Colonel Robert J. Gerard, USA (Ret.), Ph.D.
Dr. Sue Helder Goliber
Dr. Frederick F. Gorschboth
Father Henry B. Haske, S.J.
Mitchell L. Hose
Colonel James C. Hunt, Jr., USAF (Ret.)
Marie F. Keegin
Jeff Olsen
Colonel Peter B. Petersen, USA (Ret.), DBA
Dr. Robert M. Preston
Dr. William L. Portier
Colonel James W. Rowe, USA (Ret.)
Professor Thomas D. Ryan
Frederick P. Schmalberger
Dr. Frank P. Sherwood
Dr. Christopher B. Smith
Dr. Raymond C. Speciale
Dr. Ronald J. Stupak
Dudley Thompson

I also owe a debt of gratitude to the following individuals for their encouragement and support:

- Father Henry Haske, a Jesuit priest and lifelong friend, who first introduced me to Shackleton's story some years ago.

- Sandy Baumgartner, Administrator of the Mount St. Mary's MBA Program, who provided the necessary skills I lacked to see the project through. Sandy makes the hard work look easy and encourages you in the process.

- Carol Herrman, my daughter and my first editor on anything I write. Carol has a keen eye for problems of both content and writing. She was a terrific help with this book.

- Joann Woy, who did the final edit. Annie is so easy to work with and has a knack for improving your writing while still honoring the idiosyncrasies of your style.

- My children: Mark, Carol, and Cathy; and their spouses: Gail, Cameron, and Fritz. All are always supportive of anything the family does. As always, their encouragement has meant a great deal to me.

- My grandchildren: John, Brian, Katie, Matthew, Patrick, Colleen, Kelly, and Caroline. A group with absolutely no downside — they are a constant source of love and inspiration.

- My wife, Pat. Always a one-person cheering section for our family — she remains with us in spirit — always inspiring us to do our best. Her imprint is on this book as it was with earlier books. And that has improved it. God Bless!

Chapter 1

Introduction

The idea for this book came to me quite by accident. I had written three other books on leadership and was searching for a new project. I'd been turning over ideas in my mind, none of them about leadership. I felt I'd exhausted my ideas on that subject. But I was wrong!

Though there's no claim of divine intervention, this book idea did come to me at church. I was standing outside my parish church one Sunday morning, casually observing the pastor greeting people. Suddenly, a man nudged me and said: "He really has the touch, doesn't he?" And I thought: Yes, he does. Call it touch or whatever you want, but he does have something that draws people.

In the two years I'd known him, I had noticed that others also sensed he was someone special. People from other parishes often came to his services, including some of my own family.

As I drove away that Sunday, I thought: Yes, he has the leadership touch. But what is it, and what causes it?

I started making notes of random thoughts about this. I thought about the characteristics and qualities of this priest — but also about other leaders I'd known and observed during three lengthy career experiences: 29 years as an army officer, 22 years as a college professor teaching management, and 20 years of management consulting during my teaching career.

The topic would not go away. Then, one day, sitting alone in a coffee shop, the *what* of leadership touch came to me. The *how* or *why* would have to await further research. But I felt sure I would be able to define what it meant to be a leader with touch, and I knew I had a topic for a new book.

That day I began to list the best leaders I'd known. All were outstanding people who had led capably in diverse organizational settings. Most I'd be happy to work for again. But I found only a few about whom I could say: I'd fight to work for this person again.

I decided that day that I'd found a way to characterize leaders with touch: They are special people whose followers would struggle to work for them again and again on just about any project they might undertake.

Having identified a few from my own experience, I knew for certain that such leaders existed. The question became: What attributes make these people special — what is the source of their attraction?

I decided that I had to try to answer that question, and that a book project would provide the rigor and discipline needed for a careful exploration of the subject.

So — how to begin? I first performed a literature search which proved to be a dry hole. Then I considered other ideas and approaches, made many notes on coffee shop napkins, and had many false starts and dead ends. Finally, I decided on the following four-step approach:

1. Find one historical leader with a well-documented history of having this strong draw on followers — and identify the qualities that most contributed to his or her attraction. For this, I selected the South Pole explorer, Sir Ernest Shackleton.

2. Describe the attributes of six leaders from my own experience that I felt met my test for the touch: I'd fight to work for them again.

3. Seek the views of trusted others. I selected twenty-five friends and colleagues that I knew had the experience to address this issue. I defined what I meant by touch and asked them to identify a leader with touch (for them) and send me the three dominant attributes of that leader that made him or her attractive to them.

4. Analyze the information from steps 1-3, and synthesize it into a list of attributes that contribute to the leadership touch.

The following model (Roadmap of the Book: Modeling the Search for Touch) describes the approach: First, marshal the evidence of touch from the three sources (Shackleton, my personal encounter with six leaders, and the views of the twenty-five colleagues). Second, draw conclusions about the attributes and observable signs of touch from the evidence. Third, provide suggestions for actions to acquire the leadership touch — individually (through personal development) and throughout one's organization (through training).

Roadmap of the Book
(Modeling the Search for Touch)

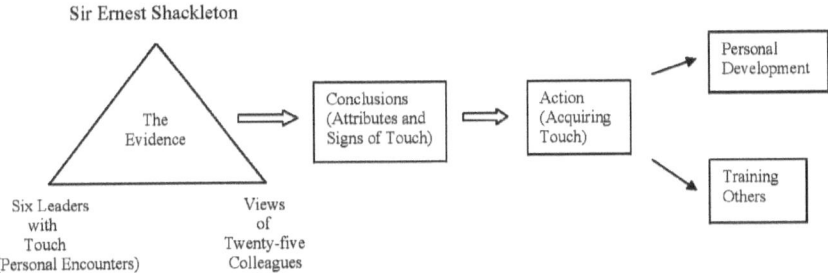

The book is thus organized into three major parts:

Part I: The Evidence: Stories and Views about Touch
Part II: Conclusions: Mining the Evidence
Part III: Action: Acquiring Touch

Each part is divided into chapters as required by the model and indicated in the Table of Contents.

An epilogue provides some final thoughts on the project — its purpose, methodology, conclusions, and its worth.

In concluding this introduction, I'd like to give you a peek at the end. What do I think I've accomplished with this book — and why should you read it?

I think the book will convince you that there is such a thing as the leadership touch, that it is a relatively rare quality, but that it can be acquired through the development and application of a specific set of attributes and behavioral traits.

The book's examples of leaders with touch will likely cause you to scan your own experience for leaders with this quality. Finding them may well inspire you to seek the touch for yourself and the leaders who work for you. And the book will guide you in that effort.

Regarding the limitations of this book, here's a bit of "straight talk." It is not a complete work on leadership traits. These are treated exhaustively in many other books, including my own earlier books. Rather, this book focuses on those special attributes that contribute most to the leadership touch. It intentionally ignores many other important attributes of leadership. Further, this book makes no claim to having all the answers to this complex matter. Leadership touch has proven to be an illusive quality and a fuzzy area to explore. But, the data uncovered persuasively suggest a set of attributes that foster this quality. Consequently, the findings here should be extremely useful to aspiring leaders — in personal development and in the training of others.

In short, this book is intended to motivate you to undertake the journey to a higher level of leadership performance — and to guide you on that journey.

Enough reason for the read!

Part I

The Evidence:
Stories and Views
about
Touch

Chapter 2

Sir Ernest Shackleton:
A Leader with Touch

Background

This is the story of Sir Ernest Shackleton (1874-1922), an Irish explorer famous for his Antarctic expeditions. For someone searching for clues to the leadership touch, there is probably no better place to look. The expedition for which he is most famous was an extraordinary leadership achievement; and his attributes were well documented in the lectures, articles, diaries, and books of the men he led. The story is convincing: Shackleton clearly had the leadership touch, and his men tell us why.

To put Shackleton into perspective, some background on Antarctic exploration is necessary, and a brief history is provided here.

Captain Robert Falcon Scott of the British Navy led the first inland exploration of Antarctica from 1901 to 1904 in an effort to reach the South Pole, but failed due to a combination of bad weather, lack of food, and illness.

Shackleton, a member of Scott's team, mounted his own expedition in 1907. His group came within 100 nautical miles of the South Pole before turning back because of a lack of food. However, this was the closest anyone had gotten to the Pole, and Shackleton was knighted after returning to England.

Scott mounted another expedition which left London in 1910, hoping to win for the United Kingdom the honor of reaching the Pole first. In this attempt he found himself in a race with the Norwegian explorer Roald Amundsen. Amundsen won that race, reaching the Pole on December

1, 1911. Scott's group arrived at the Pole on January 17, 1912, and found Amundsen's flag there. Scott and his four companions perished on the return trip.

The expedition for which Shackleton is most famous was actually an unsuccessful venture, but a spectacular leadership achievement. Briefly, Shackleton led a party of 28 men into the Weddell Sea in 1914 in an effort to cross the continent. Ice crushed his ship, the *Endurance.* His party escaped in three small boats to Elephant Island. Then he and five companions made a daring 800-mile journey by boat to South Georgia Island and crossed its glacier-covered mountainous ridge to find help in rescuing the 23 men he'd left on Elephant Island.

Shackleton's ship, the *Endurance,* left port for Antarctica on August 1, 1914. Though they would never reach the continent, their expedition has few equals in the annals of adventure stories. The expedition ended on August 30, 1916 when Shackleton rescued the last elements of his crew. Through nearly two years of inconceivable hardships and danger, Shackleton had led them with a skill that is legend. That he brought all his crew home safely is the best tribute to his leadership. Our purpose here is to discover the source of his attraction as a leader.

I've chosen not to describe here the month-to-month trials and tribulations experienced by his party or the many examples of Shackleton's leadership during the two-year ordeal. I will, however, do four things:

- List a series of key milestone events to give the reader a feel for the expedition and the ordeals faced by its members.

- Quote a few statements by Shackleton that provide insights into his leadership approach.

- Provide a number of quotations by other explorers and by Shackleton's crew, gleaned from personal diaries (written during the expedition) and from later interviews and books.

- Summarize Shackleton's leadership attributes and draw conclusions about the keys to his leadership touch.

Key expedition milestones

- The party left the whaling station on South Georgia Island on December 5, 1914, and headed for the continent of Antarctica. But it would never get there. After six weeks sailing, and within one day of reaching the continent, the *Endurance* became trapped in pack ice.

- For ten months the crew attempted to free the ship from the ice, but on November 21, 1915 the ship was crushed by the ice.

- Before the ship sank, the crew rescued five small tents, some supplies, and three open lifeboats.

- After a brief, failed attempt to march over the ice, they decided to make camp on the ice floes and wait for them to drift to open waters. For some four months they moved camp several times as floes cracked and split up.

- On April 16, 1916, fifteen months after the *Endurance* was initially trapped by the ice, the crew was able to go to sea again in the three lifeboats.

- They sailed in the open boats for a week to reach Elephant Island, a small, rocky, and dreary place. Most of the crew would be there for 5 months.

- Shackleton realized that bold action would be necessary or they would all surely perish. He decided on a very risky action: He and five others set out in one of the lifeboats headed for South Georgia Island — a journey of over 800 miles through dangerous surf and with uncertain navigation. He left his other 23 men on Elephant Island to subsist on fish and penguins.

- The journey to South Georgia Island took seventeen days, through a hurricane and rough waters. Then, when the party landed on South Georgia, they found themselves on the opposite side of the island from the whaling station.

- To reach the whaling station Shackleton and two others had to make a thirty-six hour climb over a daunting mountain range.

- They made it — arriving on May 20, 1916.

- Shackleton quickly retrieved the three men he'd left on the other side of South Georgia Island, then made plans to rescue the 23 men on Elephant Island. There were many problems. It took four tries, the final and successful one in a steamer borrowed from the Chilean government.

- They were all rescued on August 30, 1916.

A diary entry by James Francis (Frank) Hurley, the expedition's photographer, attests to the incredible seriousness of their situation: "It is beyond conception, even to us, that we are dwelling on a colossal life raft, with but five feet of ice separating us from 2,000 fathoms of ocean and drifting alone under the caprices of wind and tides, to heaven knows where."

Six decades later, Lionel Greenstreet, who had been First Officer on the *Endurance,* paid a high tribute to their leader. When asked how they had all managed to survive such an ordeal, he answered with one word: "Shackleton."

These views by Hurley and Greenstreet are explained and reinforced by the following statements of Shackleton and his men, and tributes by other explorers.

Statements by Shackleton

Shackleton once summarized his views on life and leadership as follows:

> "Some people say it is wrong to regard life as a game; I
> don't think so. Life to me means the greatest of all games.
> The danger lies in treating it as a trivial game, a game
> to be taken lightly, and a game in which the rules don't
> matter much. The rules matter a great deal. The game
> has to be played fairly, or it is no game at all. And even
> to win the game is not the chief end. The chief end is to
> win it honorably and splendidly. To this chief end several
> things are necessary. Loyalty is one. Discipline is another.
> Unselfishness is another. Courage is another. Optimism
> is another. And chivalry is another."

Another important aspect of his philosophy was his attitude toward difficult times. When asked by the headmaster of a boys' school for advice to his students, Shackleton said:

> "The only message I can think of for your boys is: In
> trouble, danger, and disappointment never give up hope.
> The worse can always be got over."

Finally, his attitude toward his men was another key factor in his philosophy and success. Shackleton once summarized the trials of his crew and his respect and affection for them as follows:

> "No words can do justice to their courage and their cheerfulness. To be brave cheerily, to be patient with a glad heart, to stand the agonies of thirst with laughter and song, to walk beside death for months and never be sad — that's the spirit that makes courage worth having. I loved my men."

Tributes by other explorers

The opinions of three famous explorers point to the magnitude of Shackleton's achievements in the field of exploration and the respect he earned from other adventurers.

- Roald Amundsen, the Norwegian explorer who was the first to reach the South Pole, paid this tribute to Shackleton:

  > "Courage and willpower can make miracles. I know of no better example than what that man has accomplished."

- British explorer Apsley Cherry-Garrard compared Shackleton to others in this revealing statement:

  > "For a joint scientific and geographical piece of organization, give me Scott; for a winter journey give me Wilson; for a dash to the pole and nothing else, Amundsen; and if I am in the devil of a hole and want to get out of it, give me Shackleton every time."

- Shackleton was also the role model for Sir Edmund Hillary, the first person to successfully climb Mt. Everest. In his book *Profiles in Audacity*, Alan Axelrod writes of Hillary's admiration of Shackleton as follows:

  > "That Shackleton failed in three attempts to reach the Pole hardly mattered to Hillary. What he admired was his ability, as a leader, to inspire his men and lead them into and out of danger. Even more important for Hillary, he saw Shackleton as a great improviser, who believed in careful planning and preparation and who was well

prepared to make a decision, but who was also willing to change his mind quickly when the situation warranted."

Statements by Shackleton's men

As we try to assess the leadership attributes of Shackleton, one of the most persuasive statements was made by Frank Wild, who served with him three times: as crew member on *Nimrod* and second-in-command on both the *Endurance* and *Quest*:

> "I have served with Scott, Shackleton, and Mawson and have met Nansen, Amundsen, Peary, Cook, and other explorers, and in my considered opinion, for all the best points of leadership, coolness in the face of danger, resource under difficulties, quickness in decisions, never-failing optimism, and the faculty of instilling the same into others, remarkable genius for organization, consideration for those under him, and obliteration of self, the palm must be given to Shackleton, a hero and a gentleman in very truth."

The following additional series of observations and tributes from his men identify important features of Shackleton's leadership approach.

> "He was a tower of strength and endurance, and he never panicked in any emergency."
>
> - Walter How
> Seaman on *Endurance*

> "There was nothing petty in his own nature. The one thing he demanded was cheerfulness from us all; and what he received from every man serving under him was absolute loyalty."
>
> - Leonard D.A. Hussey
> Meteorologist on *Endurance*

> "His method of discipline was very fair. He did not believe in unnecessary discipline."
>
> - William Bakewell
> Seaman on *Endurance*

"With all the weight of responsibility he carried on his shoulders, and all his worries — for he had many — he still found time to interest himself in an obscure scout. But he was like that; I think it was one of the qualities that made him great."

- James Marr
Boy Scout on *Quest*

"He didn't care if he went without a shirt on his own back, so long as the men he was leading had sufficient clothing. He was a wonderful man in that way; thought the party mattered more than anything else."

- Lionel Greenstreet
First Officer on *Endurance*

"Well-settled plans would suddenly be changed with little warning and a new set made. This was apt to be a little bewildering but it generally turned out to be for the good. This adaptability was one of his strong points. With him it was never a wavering between two ideas. It was a conviction that the second one was a better one and acting accordingly."

- Reginald W. James
Physicist on *Endurance*

"If he saw you alone he would get into a conversation and talk to you in an intimate sort of way, asking you little things about yourself — how you were getting on, how you liked it, what particular side of the work you were enjoying most — all that sort of thing."

- Alexander H. Macklin
Surgeon on *Endurance*

The number of available tributes to Shackleton by crew members is astounding. Those listed above give us a clue to the man and his leadership approach. But here is one more tribute by someone who was surely an expert on the subject: Frank Worsley, Captain of both the *Endurance* and *Quest*, and an individual particularly close to Shackleton. He wrote the following passage in his own book: *Endurance*.

"He was not only a great explorer: he was also a great man. Twenty-two years of his life he had devoted to Polar work — work which had brought him fame and had earned him a knighthood. He had forced his way to within ninety-seven miles of the South Pole and had returned with all his men. He had discovered the Beadmore Glacier and had added two hundred miles of Antarctic coastline to the map. He had conquered scurvy — the scourge of all explorers till his time — and had never lost a man who was under his protection. He had been the means of enabling the Magnetic South Pole to be located.

"And what of him as a man? I recalled the way in which he had led his party across the ice-floes after the *Endurance* had been lost; how, by his genius for leadership he had kept us all in health; how, by the sheer force of his personality he had kept our spirits up; and how, by his magnificent example, he had enabled us to win through when the dice of the elements were loaded most heavily against us."

Shackleton's leadership characteristics — a summary

You have already read a brief account of a remarkable expedition led by an extraordinary leader. It is an awesome task to try to synthesize the qualities of this man. But let me offer eight attributes that I think were central to his success and the source of his men's respect and affection for him. In no particular order, the qualities are as follows:

- *Ambition*: He had an achievement mentality; wanted to do big things and was restless without a project. He once wrote his wife: "I love the fight and when things are easy, I hate it." The chance to participate in a daring project of scope undoubtedly attracted many of his adventurous crew.

- *Selflessness*: In spite of his ambition, Shackleton had a remarkable lack of ego. It was always about the project, never about him personally. Dr. Macklin, surgeon on the *Endurance* wrote: "He never became the least conceited; indeed he was too big a man to ever have done so." Shackleton was also generous in his praise of his competition. After Amundsen reached the South Pole first, Shackleton cabled him: "Heartiest congratulations. Magnificent achievement."

14

- *Competence*: He knew the elements of his primary business: the sea, the Antarctic, people, fund raising. And his execution skills (a weakness of so many leaders) were outstanding. Reginald James, physicist on *Endurance* said: "Not only the main problem but its details absorbed him: food preservation, keeping sleeping bags dry, keeping stores ready for an instant shift."

- *Courage*: He needed both physical and moral courage to accomplish what he did — and he needed this quality in particular abundance to impart it to his men. There are many comments about his courage from his crew. Frank Hurley, photographer on *Endurance* said: "I always found him rising to his best and inspiring confidence when things were at their blackest." Louis C. Bernacchi, physicist on *Discovery* wrote: "He was essentially a fighter, afraid of nothing and nobody, but, withal, he was human, overflowing with kindness and generosity, affection and loyalty to all his friends."

- *Optimism*: Napoleon said: "A leader is a dealer in hope." And optimism was certainly one of Shackleton's strongest assets. His motto was "prospice," meaning "look forward." It was the title of a Robert Browning poem he loved, which said, in part:

> *No! Let me taste the whole of it, fare like my peers*
> *The heroes of old,*
> *Bear the brunt, in a minute pay life's glad arrears*
> *Of pain, darkness and cold.*
> *For sudden the worse turns the best to the brave,*
> *The black minute's at end ...*

And his actions were always congruent with this optimistic philosophy. When his ship finally sank, Dr. Macklin wrote of his reaction: "As always with him, what had happened had happened. It was in the past and he looked to the future. Without emotion, melodrama, or excitement. He said: 'Ship and stores have gone, so now we'll go home.'"

- *Loyalty*: Shackleton's single-minded focus on saving all his men is the ultimate proof of his loyalty. However, his men saw this loyalty in many of his actions during the expedition. When one of his men (Thomas H. Orde-Lees, storekeeper on *Endurance*) had a bad case of sciatica, Shackleton let him sleep on his cot in his cabin for two weeks while he himself slept on a narrow bench. Once, when hunger was overtaking everyone, Shackleton offered his breakfast biscuit to Frank

Wild. When Wild refused it, Shackleton threatened to bury it in the snow rather than eat it himself.

- *Decisive yet Careful*: Shackleton knew how to accept high risk when necessary. Of his decision to risk the dangerous 800-mile voyage to South Georgia Island he said later: "The risk was justified solely by our urgent need of assistance." But in other tight spots he had chosen to be flexible, back away from danger to live another day. He once said: "Better a live donkey than a dead lion." And his men recognized this quality and knew he would not risk them for some false bravado.

- *Integrity*: Shackleton's men obviously trusted his skill and judgment. But many of the comments recorded here indicate they also trusted the man — as a person who would be honest with them and always act in their best interest.

Keys to Shackleton's touch

In concluding this section on Shackleton, the major point to be made is that he clearly had the leadership touch. The evidence for that lies in the confidence his men had in him and their eagerness to follow him. Two final statements by his men underline this so well:

> "We were in a mess, and the boss was the man who could get us out. It is a measure of his leadership that this seemed almost axiomatic."
>
> > - Reginald W. James
> > Physicist on *Endurance*

> "He is a marvelous man, and I would follow him anywhere."
>
> > - Harry Dunlap
> > Engineer on *Nimrod*

So what was Shackleton's secret? Which of his many leadership attributes gave him the touch? Probably all of them to some degree. But after years of studying Shackleton, I've come to the conclusion that the most important thing about him that drew others to him was that he had his priorities straight: His people first, the mission second, and himself a distant third. And, importantly, his men knew it!

Chapter 3

Six Leaders with Touch:
Personal Encounters

As part of this search for attributes of the leadership touch, I scanned my own memory. During 29 years in the Army and some 20 in academia and management consulting work, I have had the opportunity to observe many fine leaders. The question I kept asking myself was: Whom would I fight to work for again? Surprisingly, there were quite a few. I credit this to particularly good luck over my working life.

In selecting six leaders for the book, I decided to pick them all from my army experience. I think it was a wise decision for three reasons: All are clearly leaders with touch; the set of six is sufficient to identify the attributes most important to me in judging leaders; and excluding all leaders in my more recent history ensures there will be no hurt feelings among many friends who I also consider to have the leadership touch.

In chronological order (listed with their rank at the time I worked for them, their position, and the time period of our involvement), the six are as follows:

Major Raymond Jones
Commanding Officer, 517th Armored Field Artillery Battalion
Germany
1952-1953

Lieutenant John Smollen
Commanding Officer, Battery C, 517th Armored Field Artillery Battalion
Germany
1952-1953

Colonel Jack A. Rogers
Commanding Officer, 69th Air Defense Artillery Group
Germany
1967

Colonel Walworth F. Williams
Commanding Officer, 3rd Brigade, 9th Infantry Division
Vietnam
1969-1970

Major General Thomas E. Fitzpatrick, Jr.
Commanding General, 32nd Army Air Defense Command
Germany
1973-1974

Major General Robert C. Marshall
Program Manager
Army Ballistic Missile Defense Program
1975-1977

The accounts that follow tell just enough about each of these leaders to explain why I was attracted to them and consider them to have the leadership touch.

Major Raymond Jones

I was commissioned in the Army in June 1951 and assigned to a field artillery battalion at Fort Carson, Colorado. In the six months I served there, I became very disillusioned as I encountered a battalion commander and several battery commanders who simply did not know their trade. Further, they did not seem to care that their junior officers surpassed them in knowledge of artillery tactics and techniques. I began to wonder if this was characteristic of the whole Army.

It wasn't — and I found that out quickly. In April 1952, I joined an armored artillery battalion in Germany. On arrival I was assigned as the junior officer in a battery that had an absolutely outstanding commander and five officers who knew and talked artillery like it was a much-loved hobby, not just an occupation.

My first week there, I was invited to lunch by Major Raymond Jones, our battalion commander, who had a reputation for knowing "absolutely everything" about artillery tactics and techniques. My battery commander

18

told me: "Major Jones fought with these same guns in North Africa; he can make them talk." And, even at this first brief meeting, I could tell I was dealing with an exceptional commander.

Major Jones had many good qualities as a leader. But what most impressed me as I served under him was his competence. For the first time, I was privileged to watch someone in command who really understood the nuts and bolts of the job, and I saw how that had earned him the respect of everyone.

In those days on the border in Germany, wondering about the possibility of a war with the Russians, we all knew that, if it happened, we were in the most capable hands.

Major Jones left after my first year in Germany, and I never saw him again. But if I'd ever had an opportunity, I would have fought to work for him again.

Lieutenant John Smollen

Same battalion — a year later. Major Jones had been replaced by a fairly weak battalion commander: not too competent and very uncertain of his status with his boss and his hold on his job.

I'm in a new battery now, with a new battery commander, Lt. John Smollen. He was terrific: highly decorated in combat in World War II, an ex-football lineman, tough looking, but funny and generous to all. He was considered one of the most capable officers, of many good ones, in the battalion.

All these things were certainly assets, and I admired him greatly. But Smollen had something much more that came to light on a field exercise.

It was winter — cold in Germany. There was a rule: No sleeping in trucks with the motor running. Then one morning one of our cooks was found dead from sleeping in the mess truck with the motor running. The battalion commander told Smollen to relieve and reduce the mess sergeant in grade for dereliction of duty.

The mess sergeant was in every way an outstanding soldier, and upon investigating the incident Smollen determined there was no way he could have prevented this incident.

Smollen explained the situation to the battalion commander, who still insisted that he reduce the man. Smollen refused and was told he would be relieved of his command if he did not obey the order.

Smollen displayed a rare degree of loyalty and moral courage. He refused to obey the order and he was relieved of his command, which predictably had an adverse impact on his career.

By biting the bullet in that instance, Smollen demonstrated a quality of selflessness that one rarely encounters in life. I knew at the time that I was unlikely to have the chance to work for him again — but I know I would have jumped at the chance.

Colonel Jack A. Rogers

Fast forward to 1967. I was a lieutenant colonel assigned to command a Hawk Missile Battalion in Germany.

On arrival I called my group commander, Colonel Jack Rogers, and asked when I should come to see him. His headquarters was an hour away.

Rogers said: "Just take command and don't worry about rushing here; I'll catch up with you." An unusual response, in my experience.

A week or so later he called and asked: "What are you doing today?" I answered: "Coming to meet you, I think."

So I walked into his office and was struck by his appearance: totally bald, ramrod straight, calm and pleasant demeanor. I was quiet — his nickel. "Colonel Hook I don't have much to say by way of guidance. I want you to know I trust the command selection system that brought you to this job. It is a tough environment. You'll be in trouble fifteen to twenty percent of the time. If you can hold it to that you'll be doing great and can expect all the right words on your efficiency report. And, if you ever get in any real trouble with me, I'll let you know. Keep your head down and go to work."

I left Rogers' office feeling totally empowered, and while I worked for him, I never lost that feeling.

He was a bit older than most group commanders, very experienced, and totally competent. He designed all kinds of tactical exercises to keep his units on their toes. His tests were so innovative they could make us apprehensive — but all his commanders loved Jack Rogers.

He became a brigadier general upon leaving the group, and I was never fortunate enough to work for him again. But a few years later I had the experience of calling him to tell him I was being assigned to command his old group. His comment: "Congratulations John, keep your head down." I should have heeded his advice better.

Colonel Walworth F. Williams

When I first met Wally Williams I wasn't all that sure I liked him and worried a bit about working for him.

In 1969, I was a lieutenant colonel reporting for a year's tour in Vietnam. I had just returned from Europe, where I had commanded a Hawk Missile Battalion. I felt pretty sure that, if I could get the right job in Vietnam, I'd have a good chance of being selected to attend the Army War College — an important milestone to making full colonel and being assigned to command a group of several battalions.

My first preference was to command a field artillery battalion in Vietnam. But that was not to be. Upon arrival in Vietnam, I was assigned as Deputy G1 of a Field Force (a personnel staff job in a corp-level headquarters).

With a heavy heart I went to meet my new boss: Colonel Wally Williams — a seemingly cheerful person whose job as Field Force G1 was to find jobs for guys like me. I told him, diplomatically and politely, that I did not want to be in a higher headquarters. I wanted to command an artillery battalion. He listened politely then said: "John, trust me you are in exactly the right place. I'm familiar with your record, that's why you are coming to work for me. Your next stop ought to be the Army War College. Working for me should help get you there."

Unconvinced, I asked him how he knew so much about me and how he had determined, with such conviction, to assign me as his deputy. Again, the smile, and: "I have good connections with the assignment people at Department of the Army, and I've been at this a long time. Trust me."

So, reluctantly, I settled in. He was a great guy. I grew to really admire him — so totally in charge of things, so cool in all circumstances. Three months after reporting to him, Williams was reassigned to command the 3rd Brigade, 9th Infantry Division — a very large, separate infantry brigade of some 7,000 men.

Before leaving he called me in and said: "You need to stay here for a couple months to help my replacement. But we'll meet again. By the way, just in case you don't get selected for the War College on your return to the States, I've set it up so you will go to the Office of the Chief of Research and Development in the Pentagon." I knew this to be a great assignment and asked: "How did you do that?" He answered: "I have connections there; used to be in that office. Friends there."

Two months later he called me: "John, how would you like to come down to the brigade for your last six months in Vietnam as my executive officer (i.e. chief of staff)?" So, down I went, knowing he was offering me one of the very best jobs for me in the whole Army.

Working for Williams in the brigade was a fantastic experience. I saw a new side of him: brave in combat, charismatic in every way, admired and respected by his men — the very same competence and confidence I'd observed, but in a much more demanding environment.

Long story short: I returned to the States in October 1970, reported to the Pentagon job he'd arranged, and days later found I'd been selected to attend the Army War College.

Williams had it all: courage, competence, confidence, integrity, plus an exceptionally deep loyalty and interest in the development and career progress of his subordinates.

Would I have fought to work for Wally Williams again? You bet I would have, in a heartbeat. Shortly after I left Vietnam he was badly wounded. He did remain in the army — and we did remain friends until his death a few years ago. Great man!

Major General Thomas E. Fitzpatrick, Jr.

In 1972, I was promoted to full colonel, graduated from the Army War College, and returned to Germany to command one of the two Hawk Missile Groups there. Those groups were part of the 32nd Army Air Defense Command, which had responsibility for air defense of all U.S. ground forces in Germany.

I'd served in that group earlier as a battalion commander, and I'd also spent a year as the G3 (i.e., Director of Operations and Plans) of the 32nd Army Air Defense Command. My group's mission was air defense of a U.S. corp of several divisions. A great job and one I felt exceptionally well prepared to undertake.

The only downside (but a big one) was the command element of the 32nd: A deputy commanding general with (trust me) absolutely no redeeming qualities — and a commanding general who was exceptionally bright but whose effectiveness was, in my view, handicapped by his personal ambition, ego, and a sort of regal complex. I worked for those two individuals for nine months, and, though I loved my job, for the first time in my service I found I simply could neither like nor respect my bosses.

Enter Major General Tom Fitzpatrick — a new commanding general, and Brigadier General Bob Lund, his new deputy. Both were outstanding people in every way — a refreshing change for the 32nd.

I'd have fought to work for either of these two officers again — but I focus here on the more senior person: General Fitzpatrick.

If Fitzpatrick had ambitions beyond this assignment, it was not apparent to me. He seemed genuinely happy with this command and determined to put his mark on it. And he did that in two ways: He brought civility to the climate in the command, and he steadily improved its tactical capabilities.

No more posing, anger, or outbursts — just a competent, firm, calm presence. That was Tom Fitzpatrick. And it worked. That tone became contagious within his headquarters and throughout the whole command. The emphasis changed almost immediately from serving the boss to serving the command.

From a tactical standpoint he also brought something special: combat command experience — a much respected quality in the Army. It is also noteworthy that his combat experience had been in field artillery, which gave him special insight into the matter of tactical support of maneuvering field army elements, which was our mission. His knowledge of, interest in, and focus on tactical operations was immediately apparent and in a very short time produced a significant enhancement of the war footing of the command. He literally transformed us from a mainly administrative posture to more of a fighting force. That change took a while to bring about, but when I left his command seven months later, the increased readiness posture was obvious.

Total competence, a quiet self-confidence, a seeming lack of ego and self-promotion, and a fair and even-handed way of dealing with everyone — these were among the many fine qualities I admired in Tom Fitzpatrick. I never had a chance to work for him again, but I would have certainly welcomed the opportunity.

Major General Robert C. Marshall

From 1974-1977, I served in Washington in the Army Ballistic Missile Defense Program Office — as Deputy Director for Planning. The program office in Washington was small (about twenty professionals) but had some very experienced scientists and some of the most talented military officers I had ever served with. The office supervised widespread command elements including a large Field Command, which directed its research and development activities. The program office was unique as the only R & D organization in the Army to report directly to the Chief of Staff of the Army. At the time I joined the program, the program manager was an Air Force lieutenant general — a highly qualified and respected individual who left soon after my arrival.

Enter Major General Robert Marshall — an Army Corp of Engineers officer who was returning to the program after having earlier commanded its Field Command in Huntsville, Alabama. I knew Marshall was a special person because the guys in Huntsville were euphoric about his taking over the program.

It did not take long to realize why. Marshall had a brilliant mind, and he probably knew more than anyone alive about ballistic missile defense.

My opinion of him as a person — never to change — was formed a week after his arrival. He made a trip to his old command in Huntsville to get briefed on the current status of things. Several of us from the program office accompanied him. He was greeted by the old-timers there with such affection and respect — it was impressive. But it was his talk to the staff there that most impressed me. He told them how pleased he was to again engage the technology of ballistic missile defense and to work with them now as program manager. During the question period that followed his talk, one person who knew him well asked: "General, does this new job mean a promotion for you?" Marshall just smiled and said: "On the contrary, the program manager's job will now be a major general position (it had previously been one grade higher). But that truly is not important to me. This is just such interesting work for me that my goal is simply to do a craftsmanlike job of running the program."

As I looked at him, I just knew: This is a guy so self-assured he does not need ego. He's not only saying promotion isn't important to him, he really means it.

I worked for Marshall for almost three years and concluded that competence and selflessness were his dominant and most endearing qualities. Later I found he could also stand a lot of heat with no loss of composure. One incident stands out in my mind. The nature of our program and the treaties associated with it placed us in a sensitive position relative to the nation's international relations. We prepared a number of reports that were scrutinized here and abroad. Many originated in my office, prepared by our staff, and signed off by me and the program manager. One day, during the time of the Ford/Carter presidential campaign, I noticed an important error in a report that, upon checking, I found had existed in those quarterly reports for over a year. A big mistake, and embarrassing. Marshall immediately went to the Under Secretary of Defense and acknowledged the mistake. He returned and called me in, calm as ever, and said: "John, they are damned mad about this; said it could impact the election." I said: "Sir, what are you going to do?" He said simply: "I just did it. Told them. Nothing else to do."

Later, he and I were riding down an elevator together and he looked at me, smiled, and said: "Who do you think they will come after on this — you, me, Ed (who wrote the report)?" "Possibly all of the above, sir." "You may be right, good night."

Nothing bad happened to anyone, but I acquired still greater respect for Marshall — some cool kind of guy!

After working for him for nearly three years, I concluded that as a boss, for me, he had no downside. In any demanding endeavor, Marshall would be the first person I would look for to team up with — a leader who clearly had the touch.

As I reflect on these six leaders, my own view of what constitutes a leader with touch — what attributes drew me to these men — comes into clear focus.

The qualities common to all of these leaders are:

- *Competence*: They all knew their job, which inspired confidence in their judgment.

- *Selflessness*: All were authentic men with a craftsmanlike approach to the job, and all placed the organization and its people and mission above their own progress. No egotists in this group.

- *Loyalty*: All felt as though they had a stake in the development and career advancement of their subordinates.

- *Empowering*: This trait was especially strong in Rogers, Marshall, Williams, and Fitzpatrick. They gave subordinates a lot of running room.

- *Courage*: All were cool in crises. Difficult times seemed to bring out the best in each of them.

- *Integrity*: All were totally honest and forthright in their dealings — a quality that led to mutual trust.

You can't go through an exercise like this and not notice in passing the bad leaders you've encountered, and why you did not like them. Thankfully, I encountered only a few really inept leaders in my career. The ones that I would avoid in the future at all costs were the self-promoters, game players, and those with volatile tempers or shaky professional integrity. Having my own share, I can easily accept most human failings, but those turn me off.

Chapter 4

Reflections on Touch: Views of Twenty-five Colleagues

The Project: Seeking input

While brainstorming ideas for this book, I had a number of conversations with friends and colleagues with extensive experience in organizational leadership and/or the teaching of leadership.

Reactions often went something like this: "Yes, some leaders do have special qualities that draw others. But off the top of my head I can't list those qualities. Maybe with some thought ….."

I found this encouraging. Maybe I was on to something. So I kept thinking, reflecting on Shackleton, my own set of outstanding leaders, and on the remarks I got from informal conversations with others. It became clear that the views of knowledgeable colleagues and friends could add depth and perspective to the inquiry. So I decided to ask for such input.

Getting reliable input would require explaining the project, defining clearly what I wanted from people, and giving them plenty of time to react. To that end, the following memorandum was sent to 30 friends and colleagues who I thought would have valuable insights to contribute:

Subject: Request for Assistance

Hi All:

I am writing to ask for a few minutes of your time.

As many of you know I have written three books in the general area of leadership — the last, "Leading at the Top: Requirements for Senior Executive

Effectiveness" in 2006. For the past several months I've been turning over a lot of ideas for a new project. I have been ignoring the topic of leadership because I thought I'd exhausted all my ideas on the subject.

But a chance event changed my mind. I am fortunate to have a very talented priest as pastor of my parish — probably the best I've ever known, as a leader. And one Sunday, standing outside the church, a total stranger pointed to this priest and said casually: "He really has the touch, doesn't he?"

This remark caused me to think back to leaders I've known — to try to answer the question: What is the leadership touch? I decided it is a worthy project — my next book!

I've tentatively concluded that the test of "touch" in a leader is that his or her subordinates would (figuratively) follow that leader off the edge of a cliff — or (literally) seek out any opportunity to stay involved with that leader in any enterprise he or she might attempt. In sum, I think leaders with the touch attract others in an unusually powerful way. Others want to work for and with them.

On reflection I also think these leaders have certain characteristics in common (I'm going to ask for your input on this). Further, I'm convinced these leaders know they have something special, and it lets them act in a very empowered way.

YOUR TASK FOR ME — IF YOU ACCEPT IT, IS: Think of the one leader you have known who you sense has the touch as I've described it (that special draw on you; you'd fight to be on his/her team) — and SEND ME THE THREE MOST IMPORTANT CHARACTERISTICS OF THAT LEADER THAT DREW YOU. You need not identify the leader.

My plan for the book is to first develop a list of characteristics by using as an example the explorer Sir Ernest Shackleton. I picked him because of one exceptional and very well documented expedition he led. Many of his people left diaries and wrote books about this expedition — so we know how his people regarded him. And he clearly had the touch as I've defined it. I'll then expand on the list and refine it using some leaders I've personally observed and by using the input you send me. Finally, I'll address the issue of whether or not "touch" can be developed. My tentative title is: "The Leadership Touch: What is it? What causes it? Why is it important? How can it be developed?"

Let me close by saying that you are on my list for this message because I very much value your opinion on this topic, due to the experiences I know you have had, and because I know you to be very reflective about those experiences.

Thank you so much for any input you choose to provide.

Best wishes always,

John

The response was excellent. Five called to chat about the project but later decided they could not come up with any helpful ideas. However, 25 provided very useful insights.

My original intent was to simply summarize the input. But the responses were so thoughtful I decided to include them in their entirety. Nearly all of the 25 have a tone that says: Yes, there is such thing as leadership touch, and here's my best effort to describe the attributes that characterize it.

As you read these 25 responses it would certainly be helpful to know the names and background of the writers. And at first I intended to provide that information. But there were practical difficulties that made this impossible and actually undesirable.

Contacted for permission to publish their input, many said they would want to revise and improve that input if their names were to be listed with their statement. I decided that such revisions would eliminate the attractive spontaneity of the original submissions. So what follows here is the full set of responses with only minor editing of a few to prevent identification of the author. I also eliminated parts of the responses that were either personal or not related to the topic of leadership. Even the format of each response has been largely retained.

That said, I still feel that some knowledge of the background of respondents, as a group, is necessary to help readers put their remarks in context. All have been friends and colleagues of mine for decades. Six are retired army colonels with combat command and high-level staff experience in the service followed by highly successful second careers in industry, government, or academia. Three have taught leadership in universities. Four others had early military service and then moved to senior-level positions in civilian life. Two participants are professors of history, and one is a professor of theology. One participant was a university provost, and four others were deans. One was the founding director of the Federal Executive Institute. Three were CEOs of businesses they personally founded. Two are directors in county governments. One is a Jesuit priest with decades of leadership and administrative experience in his order. Six have had active consulting practices, two in international consulting. One participant formed his own publishing company, and fourteen are published authors in a variety of fields to include management, business strategy, military affairs, aviation law, and marketing.

Most important, I know all the contributors intimately and know them to be both highly effective leaders themselves and keen observers of leadership in others. In short, we have 25 views here well worth listening to on this subject.

The Responses

1. Charisma. This isn't wit, attractiveness, people skills, although it can be manifested in these ways. Rather, the kind of charisma I'm talking about is magnetism. And it is ineffable. There's just something about the person that convinces you he knows where he's going. And you want to go, too.

2. Competence. The only people I've ever followed have been talented in the profession, industry, etc.

3. A sincere interest in developing you (me). Leaders with the touch spotted my capabilities and either let me fly if I was ready, or encouraged me to.

I think you have a book here.

Very interesting topic. Selecting only three characteristics will be hard: But ...

• A clear and apparent passion for goals/mission above self.

• An apparent interest in people and their development.

• Courage to do what is right and accept responsibility when wrong.

Thanks for asking.

I've given some thought, and a person did indeed come to mind. In my opinion, the three most important characteristics that drew me to this person were as follows:

1. The person demonstrated a clear PASSION for what he was doing.

2. I had absolute TRUST in the person.

3. In my eyes, this leader was the most COURAGEOUS person I knew (physically, and more importantly, intellectually).

I like the idea for this book. Please let me know how it progresses.

The three characteristics I found most prominent are:

- Competence: A very high level of skill in the arcane specifics of one's profession or trade.

- Confidence: Not only in one's self, but also in one's organization and colleagues.

- Courage: Not only physical courage but moral and intellectual courage as well.

I'm looking forward to this book.

Here goes:

- Integrity: Ability to trust him; no hidden agendas; always honest and truthful; stands up for what he believes.

- Fair: Treats all people fairly and with respect; follows rules/ procedures, but knows when exceptions can be made.

- Great communicator: Knows how to get a point across; able to communicate ideas, praise, and criticism; always has time and makes you feel that your issue is of utmost importance.

I'll try to respond in just a few words to the leadership question you posed. Never completely separable — the notion of leadership and effective management, but I'll tell you briefly what really impressed me.

1. Vision: Being able to take complex and not-well-defined "missions" and make them completely understandable and focused. This is a talent which is not given to all. This was inspirational to me. Yes, this is what we should do. Now it is clear. It cuts to the core of what we need to do for the larger, tentative mission, which perhaps began as little more than a general idea.

2. Trust: Unwavering trust in me. Really makes one try and want to succeed to show him that the trust is worthy.

3. Courage: To look in the "dark corners," to listen, to adjust, and to go where the action is to praise and commend those doing the tough work.

Am not sure the above is overly helpful but there it is!
Good luck on the book!

---

1. Trust
2. Good listener
3. Humility

I think you have come up with a great title, and it will be worth putting a book together to capitalize on it. (I know that is backward thinking, but it is my marketing side talking.) The three qualities I ascribe to a specific leader who comes to mind are: He was very bright, about his particular field and in general; he already had a proven track record of success; and he showed interest in the people who worked for him. Good luck.

Thank you for not asking for an essay.

Colin Powell has the touch.
1. Charisma
2. Integrity
3. Humility

The idea of a book on leadership touch sounds intriguing and I really think marketable. First of all, as an adult, I have never been drawn to any leader, but if I were going to be drawn to a leader it would be based on (1) the person being a winner; in essence, having a string of successes, (2) the person being a shoulder-to-shoulder leader; in effect, we jump off the cliff holding hands, and (3) the person being able to focus, set priorities, manage trade-offs, and make tough decisions; in effect, he/she must be strategically sophisticated and operationally tough.

I hope this is helpful in your efforts on the book.

Thanks for including me.

Darn! I thought about this when I got your message. Then, I forgot! No excuse. My top three are:

1. Integrity

2. Humanism: By this I mean someone who cares about you as well as your family. Someone who considers the impact of decisions on the entire organizational family. Remember the guy in New England who kept everyone on the payroll after his mill burned down (Malden Mills)? He eventually went bankrupt, but for sure, he's going to Heaven.

3. Intuition (for lack of a better word): Given a tough choice among several appealing options, this is the leader who chooses the best option. You don't know it until later, and then, in hindsight, everyone will agree that the leader's choice was clearly the best.

Good Luck! Talk to you soon.

Here are the characteristics that I think are most important for a leader:

1. Integrity: Honest, forthright, and truthful, even when it is most difficult to be so.

2. A conscientious listener: One who sincerely listens and hears the requests, the needs, the desires of his followers.

3. A person who acts in a decisive and rational way; a thoughtful and ethical decision-maker.

Sorry for the delay. I hope this provides some help to you as you begin your new project. Best of luck in this endeavor!

My first thought was a guy like Vince Lombardi; I think that is what you are looking for. My high school basketball coach was a man named Art Disque. He was like Lombardi — very tough and demanding, but a man who cared deeply about his boys. He had the knack (that I'm having trouble describing) of making you want to succeed so that you didn't feel that you let him down. It wasn't about winning or losing; it was about effort. He made you want to give everything you had. The worst punishment that you could imagine was to have Mr. Disque disappointed in you. He earned your respect because he made you respect yourself.

Hope this helps; let me know if I can provide more.

Leaders who have touched me give me the feeling they would go "over the cliff for me" or "be in my corner" to the end. I cannot let down a person like that. I feel compelled and proud to respond in kind. (I'm sure there are many different ways to say this.)

Many leaders have technical expertise, integrity, and vision but they fail as teachers and coaches. Therefore my top three characteristics are:

- Ability to teach/coach
- Loyalty
- Servant leadership approach

Don't know if this will help you, but I gave it a shot. I think the topic you have chosen is very interesting. Not all leaders have a compelling event like Shackleton, but I do think there are compelling circumstances which provide leaders opportunity to "touch" the individuals they lead.

The three most important characteristics of a leader:

1. Defining a mission, vision, and having the ability to articulate it, to communicate it effectively in such a way that subordinates realize and also understand that only by working together can this mission be achieved.

2. An "armadillo" — tough skin (ability to take constructive criticism without defensiveness) on the outside but soft underneath (kind, compassionate).

3. You mentioned "touch." I think of the French phrase: *Je ne sais quoi.* A quality or attribute that is difficult to describe or express. I think loosely translated it means: "I don't know what." One who has charisma, grace, and when he says "Come, follow me," people listen and feel good about being with and for this person.

---

1. Honesty: Honesty in a leader leads to trust; trust leads to colleagues wanting to follow the leader. Honesty promotes good judgment about what is working and what is not.

2. Vision: A leader demonstrates vision by knowing the institution, its potential and its limitations, and by knowing the vision of those being led.

3. Creativeness: A leader is creative about goals and strategies that are formulated in the context of collegial cooperation.

One person I worked for comes immediately to mind.

- He challenged me to contribute to a long-term vision of the organization — he saw a confluence of organizational goals and my interest and skills.

- He provided financial means when necessary to support the vision.

- He asked for periodic updates but left me alone to implement.

---

1. I think good leaders are people who know how to listen, and I mean *really* listen. They do not pretend to care about your opinion or your ideas on an issue; they have not already made up their minds about the issue and are just going through the motions. So they are people who ask a question and then really listen to others' ideas before formulating an answer on a policy.

2. Even if a leader has a pretty good idea what he/she wants to do, a good leader can change his/her mind after listening to people if good arguments are made or other ideas are brought up. A part of this is knowing the history of the issue (I am a historian after all!) so a leader knows the roots of the problem and understands the resistance to his/her plan. A good leader understands that there might be good reasons for such resistance and admits as much.

3. Maybe this should be #2. Good leaders can articulate the problem, summarize options, and then convince people to buy into the solution. This is done by not disparaging others' ideas, threatening, or suggesting that people who might disagree are the "enemy." They might even admit that there are many issues on which good people can disagree. Then, good leaders can set out the plan clearly, having thought about it *deeply* and recognized what must change, who will be affected, and what the costs and benefits are. And also recognize that change comes usually with pain for at least a few and not ignore that pain or pretend there is none.

4. I have to add a fourth. Good leaders have the interests of people at the core of all decisions. Not the grandizement of themselves, not even the betterment of the organization, but the betterment of the people in the organization and the betterment of the community — maybe the world! — as a whole. Some would call it servant leadership; you serve people you lead, not serve yourself.

   Don't know if this helps but I had 2 – 3 different leaders in mind when I wrote this.

Being a good academic, I can't imagine anyone — maybe Jesus — that I'd be willing to follow as unreservedly as you seem to suggest leaders are followed. But here are my three characteristics:

1. Great leaders need to be secure and strong enough to surround themselves with and welcome really strong and smart people who will generate ideas and not be afraid that if they give the leader bad news, they'll be fired or in trouble. Leaders need to listen to them. The great leader will figure out that, in the end, such lieutenants will make him or her look good. But I suspect that they're not that worried about looking good — not a bad thing — but more about getting something done.

2. In order to attract and hold the loyalty of such people — for it would not be blind, it is not enough for a great leader to be very smart and very competent and even to have a compelling vision of what needs to be done. If you're in the great leader sweepstakes, these are taken for granted. Somehow great leaders inspire trust, fidelity, and loyalty — whatever you want to call it. They are what Aristotle would have called virtuous people. They are asking you to do high-stakes things; you have to know they won't hang you out to dry as lesser people might be inclined to do.

3. One of the ways great leaders inspire trust is by conveying to you the sense that they see the whole (whatever your project is) and that's what they're about. So if they ask you to do something that you would consider against your interest, you have to be able to trust that they want you to do it for the sake of the whole that everyone is committed to. If the leader conveys to me that they only see part of the mission, the vision, the common goals, they just tick me off and I can't follow them with anything like loyalty. Leaders make you feel good about subordinating yourself and your desires and interests to something that they make seem obviously greater.

I think it's pretty hard for adults to suddenly get "character" if they don't have it. But I think intelligent and competent people who are also good in Aristotle's sense can learn to lead.

Hope this helps.

The leader I have selected to describe is Colonel Dale J. Crittenberger. I first met "Crit" when he was a major, commanding a tank battalion in Germany, and I was a captain at Seventh Army. It was primarily a social occasion and I noted he was an easy man to chat with. I next met him when I arrived at Tan An, Vietman. He was commanding the 3rd brigade, 9th Infantry Division and I was reporting to assume command of one of his battalions. We briefly renewed acquaintances, and he briefed me on operations and conditions.

After a couple weeks, he asked me if I thought we should ground the tracks since we were into the monsoon season and we were tearing up rice paddies. I told him he would have to order me to ground them because I felt their .50 caliber machine guns were too valuable. He smiled and said OK. A short time later his boss ordered the tracks grounded, and we began to airmobile.

On one occasion I was providing cover with the command and control chopper while the gunships were refueling. I told the unit commander on the ground we would have to leave to refuel but would be back with the gunships as quickly as possible. At that point, "Crit" called me and asked if it was alright if he covered while I was gone. I was surprised that he had asked rather than told me he would take over.

This was typical of the man as a leader; I didn't even know he was there. He allowed the battalion commanders to conduct operations as they saw fit and provided assistance when needed. His demeanor was always calm, and I never heard him raise his voice. He provided an example to emulate.

This was a challenging assignment. I, personally, have never found myself in a situation where I had to make such a decision about my "leader" (i.e., follow him over the cliff).

So I've considered other historical leaders who did cause their followers to give, or at least offer, their lives, out of commitment to them. Christ, Hitler, Mother Theresa, JFK come quickly to mind.

I do believe that "circumstances" at times are a factor in one's willingness to go off the cliff for a leader. Working in an office or on an assembly line rarely evokes such feelings.

Times of great import — a national emergency, a battlefield, a disaster — create the setting for such a decision on the part of the "led." What then are the qualities which cause a person to follow another through the gates of hell, if need be?

Not necessarily in order, but TRUST to me is an essential element of unquestioning loyalty to a leader. One must trust his leader with regard to the mission, the goal. Without that, he will not be followed. Please note that I take authority out of this equation. Authority, by itself, often precludes any aspect of leadership.

Another element of leadership is CHARISMA. Charisma can come in vastly differing forms: the charm of JFK, the ranting of Hitler, the sanctity of Mother Theresa. For good or evil, they were all able to create an aura that, I believe, caused a willingness, a desire to follow them anywhere.

Perhaps a final essential is DIRECTION or PURPOSE. Without one's belief or confidence that the leader knows where he's going or what he's doing, why would a follower be willing to sacrifice himself? So I guess we come back to trust.

Intriguing question! Initial thought in reflecting on this is to fall back on lessons from military leadership classes which stressed command presence, service reputation, and rapport with associates and subordinates.

Reflecting on this and your directions, I reviewed all the leaders I have served under and selected my very first squadron commander. He was a World War II fighter pilot with an outstanding combat record, and enjoyed a continuing reputation as one of the best.

He was not well educated or sophisticated, but jealously protected his authority from threats above or below. He had great rapport with the rank-and-file members of the squadron — not "one of the boys" by any means; but always available to hear complaints or accept suggestions.

He found time to regularly visit every function under his command. I'm sure he had to administer discipline, but that must have been done in private, because his most frequent expression was "GOOD SHOW." I often thought that this expression must be the key to good leadership!

Based on this and other experiences in the military and out, I would summarize the qualities necessary for the leadership "touch" as follows:

1. The certain belief, somehow held by all subordinates, that the leader will be successful in completing the task to be undertaken.

2. The leader jealously guards his/her authority yet accepts questions and suggestions about exercising it.

3. The leader interacts with associates and subordinates; displays a sense of humor and is generous with compliments and encouragement.

---

1. Integrity:

Faithful (Semper Fi)
Loyal (up and down)
Ethical/Honest/Moral
Self-disciplined
Trustworthy
Steadfast
Fair
Self-knowing
Brave

2. Competence:

Exercises correct and reasoned judgment
Technically and professionally knowledgeable
Articulate — persuasive
Decisive
Effective in organizing/delegating

3. Personal Involvement:

Provides access
Fosters bonding
Motivates ambition and performance
Fosters mutual respect (up and down)
Recognizes achievement
Compassionate

4. Charisma:

Captures popular imagination and inspires diligence and devotion; has presence and a faculty for communicating (sometimes eloquence)

I got your e-mail and think you're off on an interesting venture. But I think you are going to encounter some conceptual traps. At first I had the feeling that "touch" could be considered a synonym for charisma. That was definitely a feeling I had in the little story about the priest, who seemed to embody leadership. On the other hand, the use of Shackleton as a prototype seems to carry the "touch" much deeper. While Shackleton did show the "touch" in certain ways as I recall, there were aspects of his behavior that were not at all charismatic. It seemed that his leadership traits were most manifested when the situation really called for leadership. It was not a case of seeing someone in a general setting and exclaiming "he's got the touch."

I didn't have any trouble identifying a person who I thought had the touch: George Hartzog, who was once head of the National Park Service. As soon as I tried to identify what it was about him that constituted touch, I found I went back to more general leadership attributes. They come from a lot of exposure to him, not just an impression. If what strikes you initially is part of the touch, I would say George had a physical-psychological demeanor that said he was ready and able to take charge. Secondly, he was extremely verbal, easily able to express ideas and with considerable humor. Third, he was interested in people, and you had the feeling that this very powerful man was not inattentive to your needs.

Beyond the first impression, Hartzog displayed a number of qualities that enhanced his leadership performance. In Harlan Cleveland's terms, he exhibited "animal energy." His enthusiasm was boundless, and he was always willing to do more than his fair share to see things through. He was never tied to a desk. His great success with Congress was a function of his energy and capacity to see what had to be done.

He loved risk, to the point that he threw out all the Park Service manuals in order to free up employees to use their own ideas and initiatives. He did a great deal at the interpretive and design levels to bring a new look to the Park Service. He liked me initially because he thought I had some different ideas.

He was direct and honest. People knew where he stood. While he was very assertive in this way, there was also a humanity about him. In some cases, there was no real compromise; but in most he went out of his way to accommodate individual needs.

He was devoted to the parks; and he set high standards because of those commitments. I don't think even his worst enemies doubted his integrity.

I hope this is helpful, John. You have an interesting project on your hands. And, while I think you are going to encounter some conundrums, I think the basic idea is an exciting one.

Here are my thoughts on the qualities, characteristics, or attributes that I want my ideal leader to have:

- A transforming servant-leader committed to inspiring people to recognize their higher-level needs for the common good, not their own self-interest.

- A competent leader, but one who is open to listening to new approaches and seeks feedback.

- An authentic leader whose beliefs, voice, and actions are congruent and ethical.

- A leader who challenges and develops you, while providing the resources to support you, and makes you feel like a partner, not just like a follower.

- A self-aware leader who knows his or her strengths and capitalizes on them and continually attempts to diminish his or her weaknesses.

- A passionate leader, but one who has a calm presence in crises.

Synthesis

I think you will agree that there are a lot of thoughtful ideas in this collection of responses.

Drawing conclusions is definitely a challenge. The task of synthesizing could certainly have been simplified by providing respondents a list of attributes and having them pick from the list. It is also possible that allowing people to pick five or six attributes (which a few did anyway) might have enriched the search.

However, I wanted to skim the cream from each person's mind, unencumbered by suggestions from me. I do think this methodology accomplished that, and that the resulting spontaneity of the responses is a strength. But still, the synthesis task remains.

How to approach it? In fairness to the "synthesizer," let me say that I think it is more art than science. Once that idea is accepted, a reasonable effort can be made.

What I did was search for categories of attributes and record the number of responses that contained a reference to each category. This approach required that a judgment be made about what words or phrases would fit into each category. For example, one of the categories was competence. A number of respondents used the word *competence*, which makes for an easy call. But many others used words or phrases that reflected competence without actually using the word. Vision, creativity, confidence, judgment, track record of success—all such words or phrases can be regarded as a form of competence and thus were counted under that category. Likewise such terms as selflessness, humility, and listens to others were counted under the category I termed *authentic or lack of ego*. And such terms as supports, develops, or helps follower advance were counted under the category of *loyalty to followers*.

Using that approach, comments were classified under eight categories. The categories and the number of responses under each are as follows:

Competence	20
Authentic/Lack of Ego	17
Loyalty to Followers	12
Trusts and Empowers Subordinates	11
Integrity	8
Courage	8

Passion/Commitment to Mission	6
Charisma	5

This synthesis is, I hope, a helpful guide to the content of this collection of responses. But the methodology is admittedly imprecise. So, readers are encouraged to use both the synthesis and their own careful reading of all the responses in forming judgments.

Part II

Conclusions: Mining the Evidence

Chapter 5

Attributes and Signs of Touch

Now for some bottom lines — a synthesis of all that's gone before. It is based on my own experience, reflections on Shackelton, and the input from colleagues and friends. Diverse experiences and views, certainly. And hard to get one's arms around it all. But it is doable. Truth emerges from the data.

Recognize at the start, that these are *my* conclusions — and that they need not by *yours*. Because, what I seek to accomplish with this book is not to give you *answers* — but to pose a *question*, and suggest some reasonable answers. The intent is to stimulate your interest sufficiently so you will be inclined to think about the problem for yourself, bump your ideas up against mine, and form a personal view that will help guide you to the leadership touch.

To that end I offer a set of attributes that I think inspire followers to again and again seek out certain special leaders and follow them with trust and enthusiasm. The attributes — eight in all — are as follows:

- Competence
- Integrity
- Commitment to Mission
- Humility
- Loyalty
- Selflessness
- Good Self-Knowledge
- Charisma

Each attribute is explained in more detail in the following section. Sub-elements of each attribute are listed under the heading: *What they have.*

And the evidence or signs of each attribute are listed under the heading: *What we see in their behavior.*

Attributes (What they have)	Evidence — Signs of each attribute (What we see in their behavior)
Competence	
• Knowledge of the work of the organization • Perspective about the broader world — see the organization in context • Vision to see where to go and what must be done to get there — plus the ability to communicate it • Skills to plan and direct the effort • Good judgment in picking people and assessing events	• A high degree of self confidence • Decisiveness • Good instincts in crises and confusing situations • Sit easy in the saddle: realistic in recognizing that things can go wrong — but confident they can cope • Often have a track record of success
Integrity	
• Honest • Ethical • Truthful • Forthright/Direct • Trustworthy • Incapable of intentional deception in their own self-interest	• Guided by principles and values • Set high standards for themselves and others • Level: you know where they stand • Give and inspire trust • Demand ethical accountability
Commitment to Mission	
• Belief in the mission • Passion for the goals of the organization • Conviction that the mission can be accomplished	• Involved: have a "close the loop" mentality • Persistent in the face of difficulties • Enthusiastic • Optimistic: know and act with the conviction that anything is possible, even in the worst situations • Inspire enthusiasm and optimism in others

Humility	
• Know they don't have all the answers — or even all the right questions • A sense of honest curiosity • Always in a learning mode	• Hire smart people and empower them • Seek advice • Listen well • Flexible: can change direction based on new facts/arguments
Loyalty	
• Care about subordinates • Support and develop subordinates • Fair and even-handed • Generous with rewards • Accept their share of responsibility for failures	• Create an atmosphere of mutual trust and risk tolerance • Stay with subordinates in troubled times • Help subordinates move up
Selflessness	
• Care about mission and subordinates' welfare more than self • Not unduly focused on their own personal progress or advancement • Lack of ego	• Willing to take calculated risks • Willing to accept blame if things go wrong • Calm and inspire calm in crises • Wry sense of humor in troubled times • Hard to threaten
Good Self-Knowledge	
• Know who they are and their strengths and weaknesses • Authentic: lack of pretense; no posing or role playing	• Predictable • Consistent • Words and actions are congruent • No false pride or need to save face
Charisma	
• Ability to attract and draw others by force of personality	• Seem to have a keen sense that they have something special that draws others • Act always in a very empowered, confident manner

Looking at this imposing list can be intimidating, even discouraging. No one is likely to meet such a demanding standard.

But not to worry! These eight attributes paint an idealized portrait of the leader with touch. Reflecting back on my own set of leaders, on the input from colleagues, and even on Shackelton — I'm convinced that leaders can't possibly possess all these attributes — and that, to have the touch, they don't need them all.

Why? Because the attributes needed to meet the criteria for the touch will vary from leader-to-leader and from follower-to-follower. We may very well be drawn to a leader because of any subset of the eight attributes summarized here. But, and importantly, the closer leaders come to the ideal, the more likely they will be to draw followers by the strength of their leadership touch.

So, the development plan for leaders seeking the touch is simple to state: It is to develop and continually refine their own list of ideal attributes (hopefully helped by my analysis here). Then, to keep those attributes in sight and strive to acquire and strengthen them in practice — not in a frantic search for perfection, but in a lifelong effort toward self-improvement. We are not likely to ever reach perfection. But as we struggle toward the goal, we will develop into better and better leaders — leaders who draw followers through their touch.

Drive on!!

Part III

Action:
Acquiring Touch

Chapter 6

Personal Development

The underlying message of this book is that acquiring the leadership touch should be the goal of every leader. But, why is that important? Most leaders don't have the touch but still manage to direct organizations quite successfully. People will often follow a leader who does not have the touch. The important difference lies in follower motivation. People may follow leaders who lack touch for many reasons; but leaders with touch inspire others to seek them out, especially in difficult situations. The draw seems to be the result of some combination of the attributes of touch discussed here. And that draw is strong enough to meet the criteria for touch leadership: The follower would fight to work for that leader in any enterprise. Such a connection results in a level of loyalty and mutual trust that contributes to high organizational performance, and also to great personal satisfaction on the part of both leader and follower.

So, if it is important to strive to acquire the leadership touch, two questions remain: Can it be acquired? And how?

I'm personally convinced that the leadership touch can be acquired by most leaders who have the will to do so. And I suggest the following five-step development process:

1. Set reasonable expectations.

> Each follower has a unique set of expectations from a leader and is attracted by some subset of the attributes of touch discussed here. You, as leader, are not likely to have, to a high degree, all the attributes desired by all your people. And despite all your efforts at self-development, you may not meet the needs of all your people. But don't be

discouraged. You can train yourself to have the necessary qualities to draw many to follow you again and again.

2. *Form a frame of reference — your theory of touch.*

Theory comes in many forms but has only two purposes: to help us see, and to guide our actions. The best kind of theory for our purposes here is a descriptive model similar to the list of attributes and behaviors provided at the end of Chapter 5. I say "similar to" because that model is *my* model — it need not be *yours* precisely. What I suggest is that you start with my model and modify it based on your experience, forming your own descriptive model.

3. *Refine your model.*

To refine your initial model you must use it — look with it. Look first at your own experience, at leaders you have worked for or have had the opportunity to observe in other ways. Read the biographies of famous leaders and watch films about leaders. Test these leaders against your theory, your frame of reference. Which attributes do they have? What do they lack? And, importantly, do any of these leaders (good or bad) suggest ways that you should modify your theory? Remember that you can learn much, even from bad leaders — learn what not to do!

4. *Act/lead with your model.*

Even in its early stage your theory should be exercised — used to guide your actions. As you lead, try to model the attributes suggested by your theory. Continually improve your practices to make them ever more congruent with your touch attributes.

5. *Observe your results.*

Be reflective about your leadership practice. Observe the reactions of your people to your leadership. The best way to do that is to increase your contact with those you lead, and look for the often subtle clues that you are on target, meeting their needs and expectations — approaching, ever more closely, the leadership touch.

As you proceed through these five steps, know that acquiring the leadership touch is a never-ending process. You will always find, in your search, new leaders to observe, new books to read — leading you to an ever improving model to help you see and act as a better leader. It's not a destination; it's a journey toward improved leadership — but a journey well worth taking.

Chapter 7

Training Others

This chapter focuses on developing others — to help them become leaders with touch. It speaks mainly to leaders with touch who want to make this leadership approach pervasive in their organizations — to make touch leadership part of the organization's culture.

This is a delicate matter that needs to be approached carefully. You must be careful to avoid creating an environment in which your subordinate leaders feel you are preaching to them — that you feel you have some sort of superior approach, which they don't, but must seek to acquire. That could make you appear haughty and ego-driven, which would undermine the entire effort.

The best approach would be to never even mention the term "leadership touch." Rather, you might simply say you are establishing a program to help everyone improve their leadership approach. Also, never attempt to conduct this training yourself. Find a really good consultant to do the training. Make sure he or she is on your wave length regarding the approach and goals. And, participate in the training yourself to create an atmosphere that says: We all need this instruction, to improve individually and as an organization.

I suggest the following five-step process as one way to do this training.

1. *Have the team itself develop the theory/framework.*

    The consultant might have all participants anonymously submit a list of attributes they consider important to good leadership. This list could then be used to brainstorm toward a consolidated list that the group feels comfortable with. The attributes listed in Chapter 5 might be discussed at some point and used to refine the team's model.

2. *Have the group apply and modify the model.*

Set up a series of training sessions several weeks apart. For each session, have participants read the biography of some carefully selected leader and come to training sessions with comments on how that leader does or does not fit their model. At the end of each session, have the group revisit the model and modify it based on the comments in the training session.

3. *Focus the model on each individual.*

After several cycles with biographies, ask the participants to take the latest model update and turn it on themselves — use it as a lens to examine their own leadership approach, to see what it suggests by way of improvements. These could be submitted to the consultant with the guarantee that the information would be considered absolutely confidential.

4. *Provide individual counseling by the consultant.*

Have the individuals meet with the consultant privately to discuss their findings and plans to improve their leadership. Promise absolute confidentiality — and insist that the consultant honor that commitment.

5. *Follow up — with periodic in-house meetings.*

Schedule a leadership meeting of the participants several times a year. For each session, have everyone read the biography of some leader that the consultant suggests. Have participants use their model to critique that leader. Make the meeting a relaxed, fun occasion. Consider an evening affair with food and drink provided. Let the consultant handle the meeting and summarize important points at the conclusion. The goal: To keep your people thinking about desired leadership attributes and improving their own technique.

Epilogue

Epilogue

Now for some final reflections on this project: its purpose, methodology, conclusions, and its worth.

Suggested by the casual remark of a stranger, the term "leadership touch" intrigued me immediately. It implied an extraordinarily high order of leadership — a notion worth pursuing. Actually, it became a bit of an obsession. I felt compelled to search for its nature and causes. The commitment to a book on the subject would bring purpose, rigor, and discipline to my search. A project was born!

My definition or criteria for the leadership touch came quickly and intuitively, the result of personal reflection on some gifted leaders I'd known over a 50-year career. That criteria is: Leaders with touch have a draw so strong that their followers will fight for and sacrifice much to work with them repeatedly on any enterprise. That is the *what* of the leadership touch. The purpose of this book was to find the *why* — the attributes that produce that draw.

Regarding methodology, an initial attempt at a literature search proved unhelpful because no author had focused on my specific criteria. I quickly concluded that only original research would suffice. It would be necessary to find followers who felt this strong attachment to certain leaders, and to find out why (i.e., the attributes that attracted them).

Three research sources were selected: Shackleton, my own six examples of leaders with touch, and the opinions of twenty-five friends and colleagues. These sources produced a rich collection of attributes contributing to the leadership touch.

Developing conclusions from all the data was a challenge. The task proved to be more art than science, and the resulting synthesis may not have the precision and certitude we'd all prefer. However, I feel the conclusions have advanced us considerably in the search for the ingredients of the leadership touch. If you have doubts about that, let me offer just a bit more confirming evidence.

Recently, I listened with interest to a television interview with the renowned presidential historian, Doris Kearns Goodwin. Asked about the qualities she had found important to being a great president, she mentioned ten:

- Put diverse people on their team
- Had gone through adversity with grace
- Possessed emotional intelligence
- Shared rewards with others
- Projected warmth
- Were willing to acknowledge mistakes and learn from experience
- Controlled their emotions
- Had ambition without ego
- Knew how to relax
- Reached out to opponents

Goodwin's list was encouraging in that it agreed quite well with the book's conclusions. The terminology was a bit different, but the meaning was very similar.

I also found, on a dusty bookshelf, a book by the distinguished soldier-journalist General S.L.A. Marshall. Marshall first enlisted in the Army during World War I and served as an army combat historian in World War II, Korea, and Vietnam. He wrote a number of books on military operations and leadership. His most famous book was *Men Against Fire* written in 1947. The book I found was *The Officer as a Leader*, which was written in the 1960s and provides a synthesis of all he had learned about leadership covering the various wars.

In his book, Marshall writes of asking a group of famous colleagues the question: What is the one indispensable requirement of the true leader? The answer was: "It is the ability to carry out an assigned task and do it completely; the committing of one's self to the closing of the circuit." This sounded like a vote for competence and commitment to mission — thus a match with this book's conclusions.

Near the end of his book, Marshall wrote what seems to be an attempt to capture what he had personally found to be the most important leadership attributes:

Quiet resolution.
The hardihood to take risks.
The will to take full responsibility for decisions.
The readiness to share rewards with subordinates.
An equal readiness to take the blame when things go wrong.
The nerve to survive storm and disappointment and to face toward each new day with the score sheet wiped clean, neither dwelling on one's successes nor accepting discouragement from one's failures.

In these things lies a great part of the essence of leadership, for they are the constituents of that kind of moral courage that has enabled one man to draw many others to him (read: "touch") *in any age.*

This is nearly a perfect match with the findings of this book. Think: integrity, humility, loyalty, selflessness. I left the reading of this passage more convinced than ever that my efforts on this book were worthwhile and that the conclusions are quite valid.

So, what was accomplished — what does my book provide? I think two things.

- Sufficient stories about leaders with the touch and diverse views on the nature and importance of touch to convince most readers that there is such a phenomenon as the leadership touch and to inspire a desire to acquire it.

- A set of attributes that contribute to the leadership touch, and an action process to develop those attributes — to acquire the leadership touch.

And, was it worthwhile? I hope so, and I think so. Granted there are countless books on leadership and nearly all of them can help us improve. But this book does extend the discussion to quite a high order of leadership — a capacity worth seeking.

By whom? By just about everyone, in my view. When considering an audience for a book like this there is a temptation to think of its relevance to those in formal organizations in industry, government, and the non-profit sector. But that ignores the informal leadership roles people play in organizations and the demand for leadership in so many other areas of our lives: our schools, churches, volunteer activities, athletics, and other avocations. And let's not forget perhaps our most important organization: the family. Life throws us many curve balls, and few families avoid crises. When they come, all members have a role and responsibility in helping one another respond by providing leadership through the crisis.

Bottom line: leadership matters. And we all lead. Doing it well is our task, our obligation to ourselves and others. The journey to the leadership touch is a move toward excellence. Acquiring the touch is possible, and the journey is well worth taking. The purpose of this book is to help you in that journey.

Appendix:

Selected Literature and Films on Leadership

Leadership Concepts

Bennis, Warren. *Why Leaders Can't Lead*. San Francisco: Jossey-Bass, 1989.

Bennis, Warren. *On Becoming a Leader*. New York: Addison-Wesley, 1989.

Bennis, Warren, Gretchen M. Spreitzer, and Thomas G. Commings. *The Future of Leadership: Today's Top Leadership Thinkers Speak on Tomorrow's Leaders*. San Francisco: Jossey-Bass, 2001.

Blanchard, Ken. *Leading at a Higher Level*. Upper Saddle River, New Jersey: Prentice Hall, 2007.

Bossidy, Larry and Ram Charan. *Execution: The Discipline of Getting Things Done*. New York: Crown Business, 2002.

Boyatzis, Richard and Annie McKee. *Resonant Leadership*. Boston: Harvard Business School Press, 2005.

Collins, Jim. *Good to Great*. New York: Harper Collins, 2001.

Daniels, Aubrey D. and James E. Daniels. *Measure of a Leader*. New York: McGraw Hill, 2007.

Drucker, Peter F. *The Executive in Action*. New York: Harper Business, 1996.

Harvard Business Review on Leadership (A collection of articles). Boston: Harvard Business School Press, 1998.

Harvard Business Review on the Mind of the Leader (a collection of articles). Boston: Harvard Business School Press, 2005.

Maxwell, John. *The 360° Leader.* Nashville: Thomas Nelson, 2005.

Leading Change

Harvard Business Review on Leading Through Change (A collection of articles). Boston: Harvard Business School Press, 2006.

Harvard Business Review on Change (A collection of articles). Boston: Harvard Business School Press, 1998.

Johnson, Spencer. *Who Moved My Cheese?* New York: G.P. Putnam's Sons, 1998.

Kotter, John P. and Dan S. Cohen. *The Heart of Change.* Boston: Harvard Business School Press, 2002.

Kotter, John P. *Leading Change.* Boston: Harvard Business School Press, 1996.

Leading in Crises

Alexander, Caroline. *The Endurance: Shackleton's Legendary Antarctic Expedition.* New York: Knopf, 1998.

Axelrod, Alan. *Profiles in Audacity.* New York: Sterling, 2006.

Giuliani, Rudolph W. *Leadership.* New York: Miramax Books, 2006.

Kennedy, Robert F. *Thirteen Days: A Memoir of the Cuban Missile Crisis.* New York: W.W. Norton, 1969.

Morrell, Margot and Stephanie Capparel. *Shackleton's Way: Leadership Lessons from the Great Antarctic Explorer.* New York: Penguin Books, 2001.

Nathan, James A. *The Cuban Missile Crisis Revisited.* New York: St. Martin's press, 1992.

Thomas, Evan. *Sea of Thunder: Four Commanders and the Last Great Naval Campaign 1941-1945.* New York: Simon and Schuster, 2006.

Leaders in Action

Goodwin, Doris Kearns. *Team of Rivals*. New York: Simon and Schuster, 2005.

Hayward, Stephen F. *Churchill on Leadership*. Rocklin, California: Prime Publishing, 1997.

Larrabee, Eric. *Commander in Chief: Franklin Delano Roosevelt, His Lieutenants, and Their War*. New York: Harper and Row, 1987.

McCall, Morgan W., Michael M. Lombardo, and Ann M. Morrison. *The Lessons of Experience*. Lexington, Massachusetts: Lexington Books, 1988.

Noonan, Peggy. *John Paul the Great*. New York: Penguin Books, 2005.

Reeves, Richard. *President Kennedy*. New York: Simon and Schuster, 1993.

Reeves, Richard. *President Reagan*. New York: Simon and Schuster Paperbacks, 2005.

Teaching Leadership

Parks, Sharon Daloz. *Leadership Can Be Taught*. Boston: Harvard Business School Press, 2005.

Suggested Films for Leadership Training

Apollo 13 (Story of crisis at NASA)

Iacocoa (An NBC White Paper on the CEO, narrated by Tom Brokaw)

In Harms Way (Naval Leadership in World War II)

The Endurance (One of several films on the leadership of Sir Ernest Shackleton during his famous Antarctic expedition)

The Missiles of October (Story of the Cuban Missile Crisis)

Thirteen Days (Story of the Cuban Missile Crisis)

Twelve O'clock High (World War II study in command)

About the Author

Dr. John Hook was fortunate to have three diverse career experiences contributing to his background in leadership: an army officer for 29 years, academic for 22 years, and management consultant throughout his teaching career. In the Army, he commanded units from 100 to 3,500 men; served in three different research and development agencies in Washington; taught at West Point; and chaired the Command, Leadership, and Management Department at the U.S. Army War College. After retiring from the Army in 1980, he chaired the Business and Economics Department at Mount Saint Mary's College (now University) for 12 years, then remained a faculty member there for an additional 10 years. During that time, he also conducted hundreds of management seminars and provided other consulting services for public, private, and non-profit organizations, most for senior-level leaders. He has published three other books on management and leadership: *The Agile Manager's Guide to Influencing People; Developing Executive Skills: Managing Yourself, Others, and Organizations;* and *Leading at the Top: Requirements for Senior Executive Effectiveness.* He is Professor Emeritus of Management at Mount St. Mary's University in Maryland.